A Marriage Tip Book

A Marriage Tip Book

the wise ones
of the
Second Grade Class

LUCKY VALLEY PRESS
CARMEL CALIFORNIA

© 2014 Dr. Jerry Traynor & Nan Heflin
All rights reserved

Original Tip Book
from the collection of
Dr. Jerry Traynor & Nan Heflin

Book & Cover Design by Ginna BB Gordon

ISBN: 978-0-9856655-8-6

No part of this book may be reproduced in any
form by any electronic or mechanical means,
including photocopying, recording, or information
storage and retreival without the express
permission of the publishers

Lucky Valley Press
Post Office Box 5474
Carmel-by-the-Sea CA 93921
WWW.LUCKYVALLYPRESS.COM

Printed in the United States of America

Foreword

When we married in April, 2008, one of the most precious gifts we received was from a class of second graders, whose beloved teacher had asked them each to draw a picture with a marriage tip for the new couple.

We found their thoughts on love and relationships to be fresh and timeless. We offer you the wisdom of the second grade class.

May you enjoy a long and beautiful life, filled with joy and happiness and all that comes from loving deeply.

Nan Heflin & Dr. Jerry Traynor

Publisher's Note

Today, marriage is inclusive, and the true meaning remains: a devoted loving relationship.

We chose to publish this book because of the simplicity and clarity of the messages from the minds and hearts of a group of second graders.

When looking at the drawings with focus, it is wonderful to see the complexity of some, showing the thought processes of the children.

Zoom in with your eye to see the stick figures holding hands, the clean laundry on the line, the woman with breakfast in bed, the diamond ring.

Count the chairs around the table in the restaurant, notice the candles and bride and groom on the wedding cake.

The wise ones have created the perfect gift - straight from their hearts - to establish a good and lasting partnership.

Enjoy *A Marriage Tip Book* and, remember to "use school rules."

Ginna BB Gordon
David J Gordon
Lucky Valley Press
Carmel CA, 2014

Buy a wedding ring.

Giorgio

Remember, get the jewelery first then get the wedding cake.

Paloma

John

 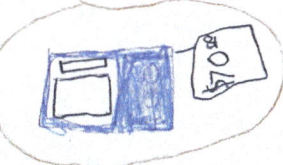

Buy what you really need, don't overspend.

Christie

Share the work often and trade once and a while so you don't keep the same work.

stijn

Dear Ones, ♡ Don't forget each others Birthdays.

Noah

try to get along.

Dear Ones, remember to get a wedding gift!

Love,
Cormac

Ethan

Try not to fight with her a lot, P.S. That might turn into a bad thing.

Remember to get your favorite food to go.

Gregory

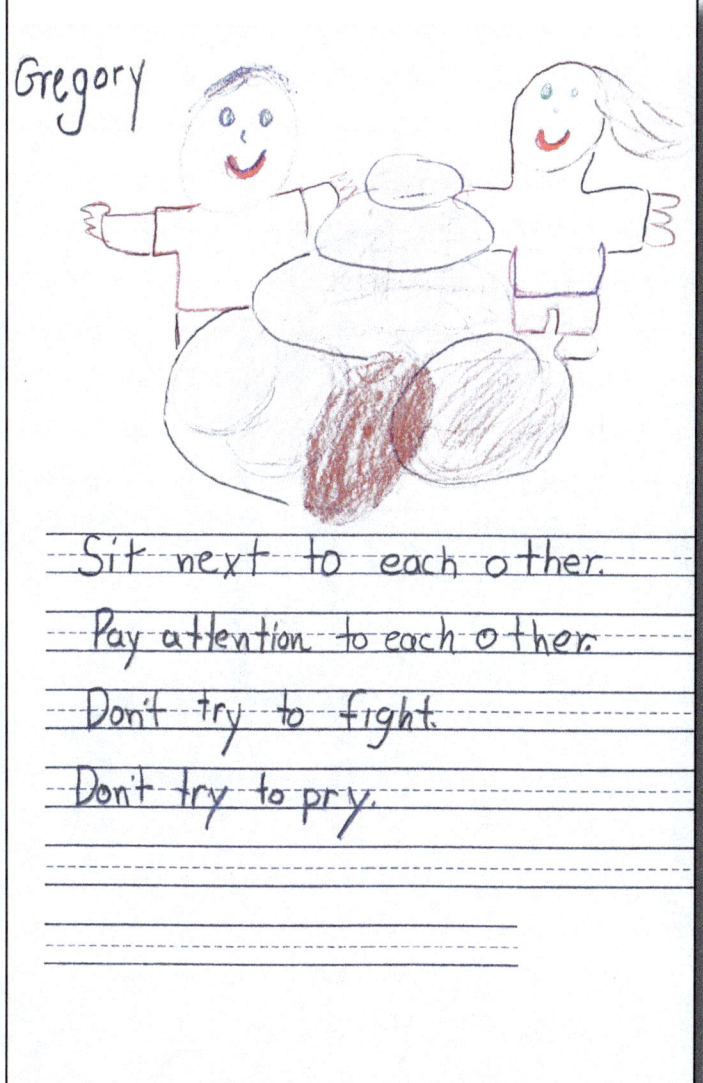

Sit next to each other.
Pay attention to each other.
Don't try to fight.
Don't try to pry.

Outside

Cheese pizza!

Fruit salad!

Have a family dinner at a restaurant.

FOOD BURNED!

zackary

Make shure you talk it out and try to agree with echuther.

from Matthew

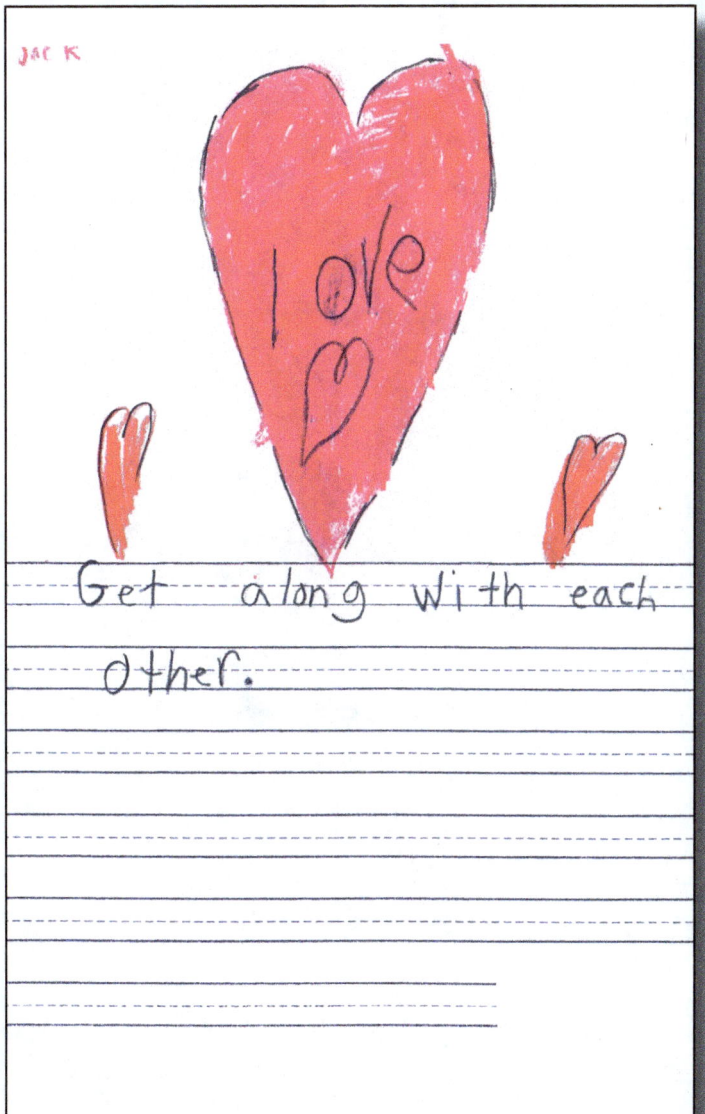

Get along with each other.

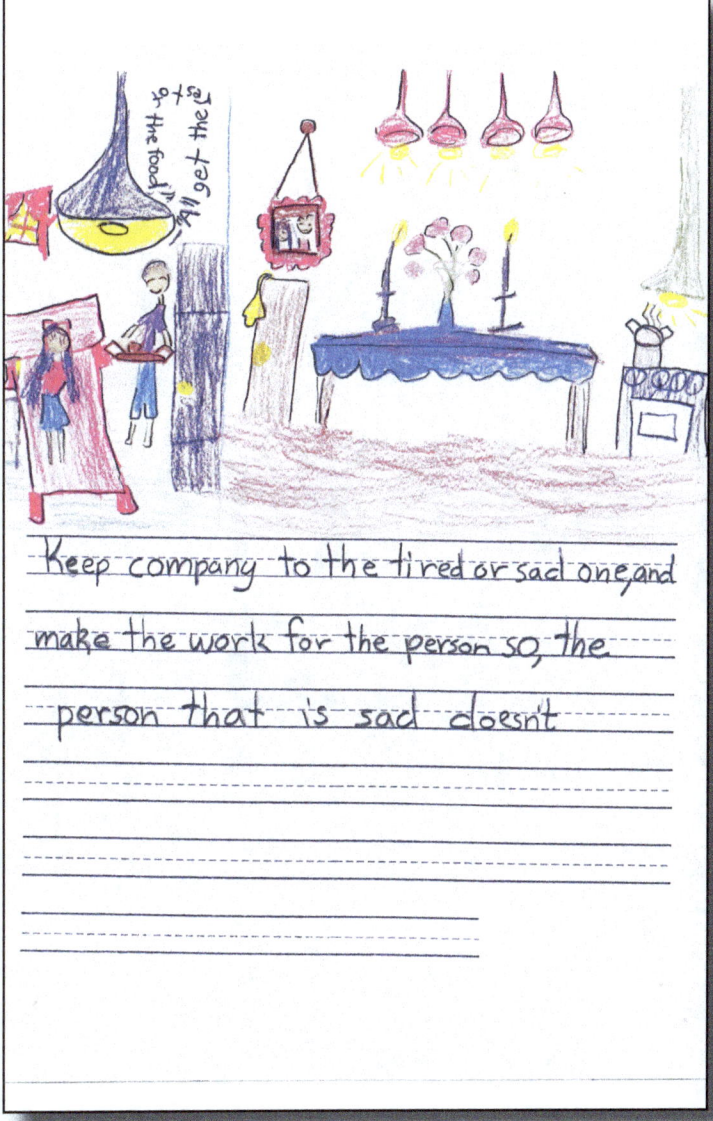

Keep company to the tired or sad one, and make the work for the person so, the person that is sad doesn't

Johnny

Love

Spend time together.

Dear Ones, remember to be nice each other.

Dear Ones, share the money equally.

Isabella

Hold hands.

Stay Happy and help her be happy. Suggesten! Take a deep breath in for four seconts beath out for 6 seconts.

Use school rules.

with love from

the wise ones

*Our Thanks
to the Wise Ones
of the
Second Grade Class*

Created with love
by
WWW.LUCKYVALLEYPRESS.COM
Carmel California USA

www.ingramcontent.com/pod-product-compliance
Lightning Source LLC
Chambersburg PA
CBHW070100020526
44112CB00034B/2119